# −Fast Tracks

# −Off Road Racing

A.T. McKenna

Published by Abdo & Daughters, 4940 Viking Drive, Suite 622, Edina, Minnesota 55435.
Copyright © 1998 by Abdo Consulting Group, Inc., Pentagon Tower, P.O. Box 36036, Minneapolis, Minnesota 55435 USA. International copyrights reserved in all countries. No part of this book may be reproduced in any form without written permission from the publisher.

Printed in the United States.

Cover and Interior Photo credits: Allsport USA, Duomo, SportsChrome

Edited by Paul Joseph

Library of Congress Cataloging-in-Publication Data

McKenna, A. T.
   Off road racing  / A. T. McKenna.
      p.   cm. -- (Fast tracks)
  Includes index.
  Summary: Describes the nature, vehicles, and competitions of off-road racing, focusing on four-wheel drive race vehicles such as Range Rovers, Landcruisers,and Jeeps.
  ISBN 1-56239-833-4
  1. All terrain vehicle racing--Juvenile literature.  [1. All terrain vehicle racing.  2.All terrain 2vehicles.]  I. Title  II. Series: McKenna, A. T. Fast tracks.
  GV1037.M35  1998
  796.7'2--dc21
                                                           97-51445
                                                               CIP
                                                                AC

# Contents

# −Off Road Racing

*Off-road* racing is becoming a popular type of racing across the world. Off-road racing is very different from other forms of racing. It involves racing across the countryside where there is no track. Drivers learn to drive through rugged land, which is many times muddy and slippery.

There are two categories of off-road racing. One type is timed races that run against the clock. The driver who finishes with the quickest time wins the race.

The other type of off-road race is like an obstacle course. The race is not timed. The driver who completes the race with the least amount of penalty points wins. Some believe that off-road racing is good practice for other types of racing. After all, if you can make it through a jungle or desert without a road, racing on a track should be simple, right?

Getting started in off-road racing doesn't require a lot of money like other types of auto racing does. There is no need to buy a certain race vehicle to race. Many off-road racers already have the vehicle they are racing—it's their regular four-wheel drive vehicle that they drive everyday!

*Off-road vehicles come in all shapes and sizes.*

# –What is Four Wheel Drive?

*Four-wheel* drive means that the power from the engine is sent to all four wheels of the vehicle. In regular two-wheel drive cars that are driven on the road, the engine power is just sent to two of the four wheels—front-wheel drive or rear-wheel drive. The other two wheels just turn freely, with no power.

With a four-wheel drive vehicle, the vehicle can pull on the front two wheels and push on the rear two. This is helpful when bouncing over rocks or bumps in the road to prevent losing control of the vehicle.

The very first four-wheel drive vehicle was designed in 1908, by the Four Wheel Drive Auto Company in Clintonville, Wisconsin. Other companies built four-wheel drive vehicles before that, but didn't put them into production. They just made one or two.

The Jeep was the first mass-produced four-wheel drive vehicle. During World War II, there was a need for a utility vehicle for the American Army in Europe.

A company named Willys Overland won the contract and produced a vehicle that the Army called "G.P.," meaning "general purpose." A soldier started calling the vehicle "jeep" and the name stuck. Today, the Jeep, made by American Motor Corporation (AMC) is still one of the most popular four-wheel drive vehicles.

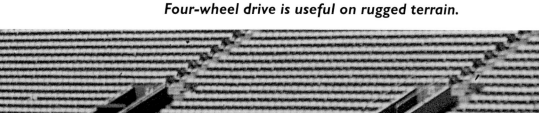

**Four-wheel drive is useful on rugged terrain.**

# −Road Taxed Vehicle

*Road* Taxed Vehicle (RTV) racing is for drivers who are just starting to race. Sometimes this is called the "grassroots" competition level, before moving to professional driving.

Drivers race normal road vehicles such as Range Rovers or Jeeps. An RTV race is not against the clock. This is no speed event. What is most important in this type of racing is both the vehicle's and the driver's ability to endure the race.

At the race site, the officials mark off a series of short routes between a pair of canes. These canes look like thin poles and are called "gates." There are between 10 and 12 gates per section. The driver must drive the distance between each of the gates without stopping or touching any of the canes. The position of the canes is not easy to maneuver.

The canes are placed at difficult points where the land is hilly or rocky. Drivers must use all their skills just to get past the canes. The canes are numbered in descending order, from 10 or 12 to zero. If the driver gets through the first seven pairs of canes, but hits the canes at the next gate, the driver will have three penalty points.

Drivers have a score card on which the penalty points are marked for each section. Once drivers finish a section, they move

on to the next section which will have 10 or 12 more gates. At the end of the day, the driver with the lowest score (least amount of penalty points) wins. After a driver has competed for a while in RTV racing, there is an experts class that has more difficult courses and it is much more competitive.

In order to compete in RTV off-road racing, drivers must pass inspection on the day of the race. Most of the requirements are for the safety of the driver and other drivers in the race. Requirements will vary depending on the type of off-road race.

Some of the general requirements include having the front windshield securely attached to the body of the car. The rear windshield may be open. The vehicle must have the hard top of the vehicle securely attached.

All drivers must show a valid driver's license and club membership card if it is a club event. Vehicles must have their normal road tires on for RTV competition. These tires must be the ones that were on the car when the driver arrived at the race. The vehicle must have the original wheels on too.

Seatbelts must be worn. There is no smoking allowed by the drivers. Lastly, all vehicles are usually required to have towing equipment mounted on the car in case the car has to be towed.

# –Competition Safari

*Competition* Safari is another kind of off-road racing. This type of racing is for speed. Drivers race against the clock over a course of eight to ten miles. Drivers must race the course a number of times. It isn't a one time only race. The drivers must prove that they have the skill and their vehicles are reliable enough to make it through the course several times. The driver with the best average time wins.

Since Competition Safari racing is more dangerous, drivers are required to have a roll bar on the car. The roll bar is an upside down "U" shaped bar that is very strong and is padded with foam to protect the driver's head. It is required to be several inches above the driver's helmet. If a car crashes and flips over during a race, the weight of the car will be on the roll bar, not the driver.

A fire extinguisher is also required for Competition Safari racing. It is placed near the driver's seat. If there is a fire in the engine, the driver must be able to reach the fire extinguisher and try to put out the fire.

*Opposite page: Competition race cars must have a roll bar to protect the drivers.*

# –Expedition Off Road Racing

**Besides** RTV and Competition Safaris, there is another kind of off-road racing that is believed to be the toughest. This is called Expedition Racing. An expedition is a journey taken by an organized group of people.

Drivers are pushed to the limit in a test of endurance over several days and thousands of miles.

These races are for those who have been off-road racing for a long time and are experienced with surviving in the wild. These races can take place in many places across the world, including deserts, mountains, bodies of water, and jungles.

Some expedition off-road races include all of the above throughout the race course! Therefore, it's an obstacle course for only the most experienced off-road racer. There are several famous off-road races all over the world.

The Camel Trophy is one type of off-road race that is called an expedition race. Every year thousands of off-road drivers apply to enter the Camel Trophy. Only two amateur drivers are taken from each country. There are about 15 countries involved in the Camel Trophy. This race is not in a set area of the world every year. Different sections of the world are selected and drivers compete for 1,000 miles.

Some of the areas on which the Camel Trophy has been held are Brazil, Sumatra, Papua-New Guinea, Zaire, Borneo, Australia, Madagascar, and Indonesia. In the Camel Trophy, racers drive through land where there is no civilization. It is believed that some of this land has never been traveled by humans before. Probably the toughest part of the Camel Trophy is crossing the rivers that drivers encounter.

The very first Camel Trophy was held in the Amazon Basin in Brazil in 1980. The group of Germans who competed in this first race used specially prepared Jeeps. Now drivers use Range Rovers and Land Rovers. All the vehicles used in the Camel Trophy are not made specifically for the race. They are production vehicles (driven on the streets everyday) with some minor changes.

There is a trophy for the winner of the race, which is based on the performance of various tasks during the race. There is also a Team Spirit prize. This award is the most prized, and is decided by all the race teams. This award goes to the team that best represents the spirit of the Camel Trophy by keeping the best attitude and spirit throughout the race.

*Expedition racers preparing for the big race.*

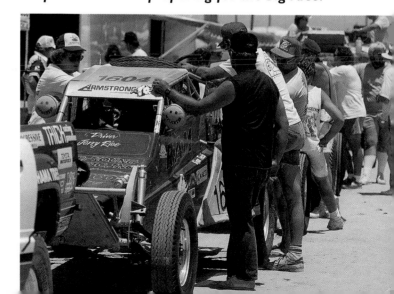

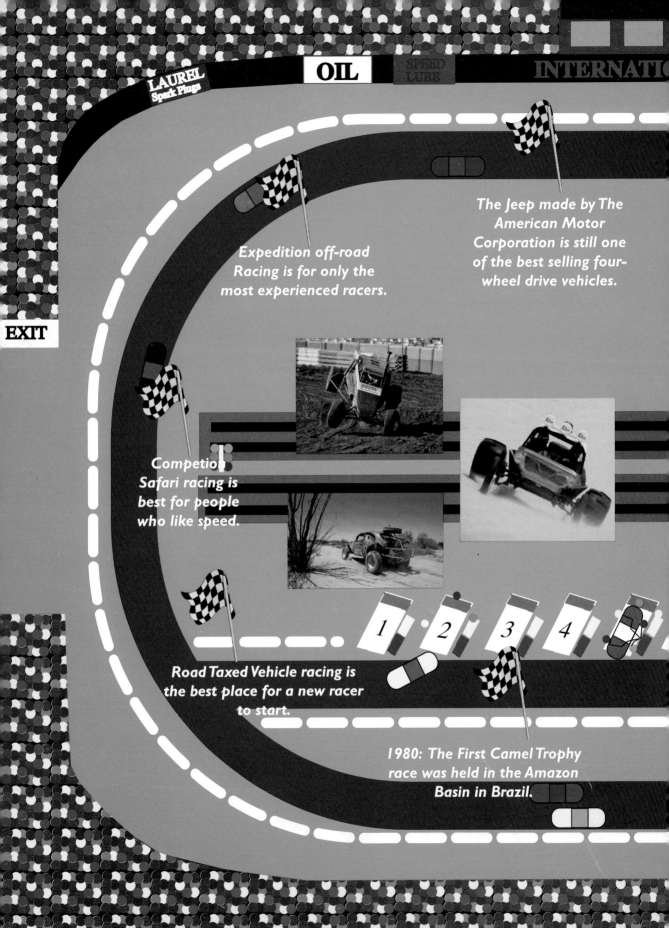

LAUREL
Spark Plugs

OIL

SPEED
LUBE

INTERNATIO

EXIT

Expedition off-road
Racing is for only the
most experienced racers.

The Jeep made by The
American Motor
Corporation is still one
of the best selling four-
wheel drive vehicles.

Competiton
Safari racing is
best for people
who like speed.

1   2   3   4

Road Taxed Vehicle racing is
the best place for a new racer
to start.

1980: The First Camel Trophy
race was held in the Amazon
Basin in Brazil.

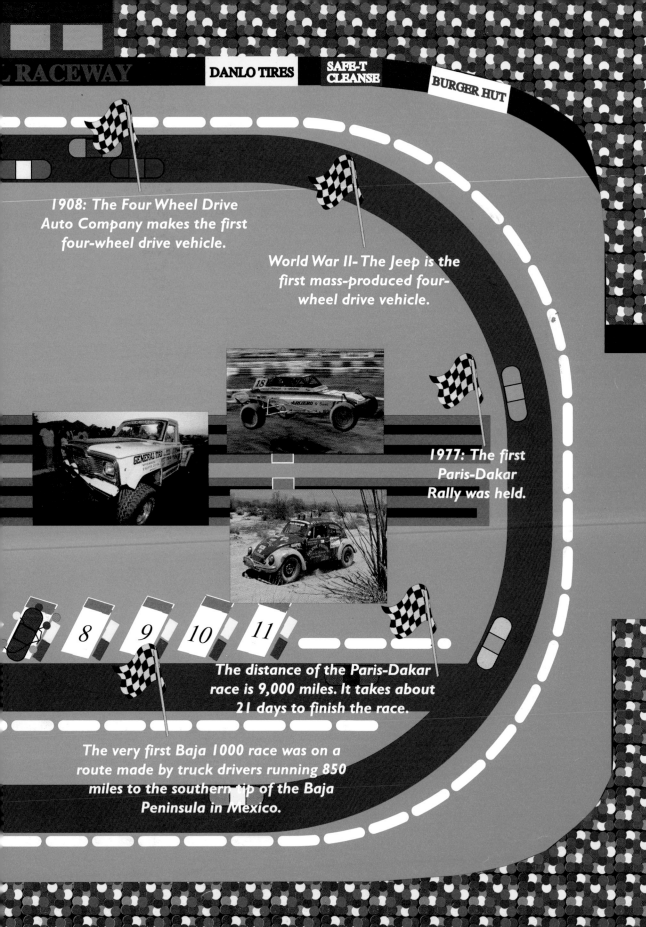

DANLO TIRES

SAFE-T CLEANSE

BURGER HUT

**1908: The Four Wheel Drive Auto Company makes the first four-wheel drive vehicle.**

**World War II– The Jeep is the first mass-produced four-wheel drive vehicle.**

**1977: The first Paris-Dakar Rally was held.**

8  9  10  11

**The distance of the Paris-Dakar race is 9,000 miles. It takes about 21 days to finish the race.**

**The very first Baja 1000 race was on a route made by truck drivers running 850 miles to the southern tip of the Baja Peninsula in Mexico.**

# –The Paris-Dakar Rally

*Of* all the international off-road races, The Paris-Dakar Rally is probably the toughest. The race was started by Frenchman Thierry Sabine. This race starts in Paris and ends on a beach in West Africa.

The distance of the race is 9,000 miles. It takes about 21 days to finish the race. The first Paris-Dakar Rally was held in 1977. This race requires a team of mechanics, a fleet of off-road vehicles (usually two to three), a couple of drivers and plenty of money!

Off-road racing teams for this event usually have two competitive vehicles and a third vehicle that serves as a support service truck. The support service truck carries all the spare parts and medical assistance if needed. But since service vehicles are not permitted in the Paris-Dakar Rally, the third vehicle also has to compete in the race.

In the Paris-Dakar Rally there are three classes. The Marathon Class is for two or four-wheel drive vehicles that are on sale to the public. This means that the vehicles are being driven on the streets everyday, like Range Rovers and Landcruisers. The only changes allowed are adding some safety equipment and minor work on the suspension.

The suspension is made of springs, shock absorbers, and other parts that protect the vehicle from the rough ride that comes from the wheels. Improving the suspension will give the driver a smoother ride. This class is very hard to compete in, since teams are not allowed to change pieces of the vehicle to make it more competitive.

The next class is Improved Production. This means that the team has to use a standard production vehicle, but the team is allowed to make major changes to the vehicle. Once all the changes are made, the vehicle will look similar to vehicles on the road, but will be much faster and more powerful.

The third class is called the Prototype Class. This is the class that usually produces the winner of the Paris-Dakar Rally. A prototype is an original, unique vehicle. This class allows the team to change the body of the vehicle, the engine, and the transmission. Most teams start with a drawing board, designing on paper what they want the vehicle to look like.

*The Paris-Dakar is one of the most grueling races in the world.*

# –The Baja 1000

**One** of the most well-known off-road races is the Baja 1000. "Baja" comes from the Spanish word meaning below. Drivers race on 1,000 miles of dry desert, rugged mountains, and the Mexican coastline.

The Baja 1000 is such a difficult off-road race, that less than half of the cars finish the race. The race starts and finishes on paved highway, but the distance in between is unpaved desert. Those who participate in this difficult race have to deal with rocks that can rip tires, flying sand that can blind the drivers, and sizzling hot temperatures that can overheat engines. Plus, the race goes on night and day, so drivers have to be alert at all times.

The very first Baja 1000 race was on a route made by truck drivers starting in the north and running 850 miles to the southern tip of the Baja Peninsula in Mexico. But before there was a race, people used to come to this area to test their cars off road. They mapped out their own routes that went along the white sandy beaches of the Pacific Ocean.

Since the Baja desert is very harsh on regular cars, these adventurous people had to install oversized tires, heavy-duty clutches, extra shock absorbers, and more.

The beautiful Mexican desert is a very scenic spot for a race. Drivers drive past boojum, which are desert plants that are only found in this part of the world. These plants are the oldest living organisms in the Baja desert. Some are 600 years old.

Another site to see includes polar bear rock, which is a rock formation that looks just like a polar bear. Drivers in the Baja 1000 know how far the finish line is from polar bear rock. The scenic mountains are home to many animals, including deer, mountain sheep, and deadly cougars. Then there is the Pacific Ocean, home to more than 800 species of fish.

There are eight check points along the Baja 1000 race course. Drivers can refuel, replace parts, and relax for a few minutes. These are the only spots to get spare parts. If drivers break down out in the desert, away from a check point, they sometimes have to wait a long time for help. Someone will eventually come along to help out, but usually the driver will lose too much time to finish the race.

**Less than half the vehicles in the Baja 1000 actually finish the race.**

# —Building Off Road Vehicles

*All* off-road racing vehicles are four-wheel drive vehicles. They do not look like race cars. In fact, they are usually vehicles such as Land Rovers, Toyota Landcruisers, Jeeps, and Mercedes Unimogs. From the outside, off-road racers look much like many of the vehicles being driven on the streets everyday. However, off-road vehicles don't look much like a regular vehicle once you look inside.

Some of the main components on a off-road race car are the chassis and the body. The chassis looks like the skeleton of a car. The chassis consists of several pieces of steel welded together to form a frame for the car. All sharp edges on the chassis must be smoothed before putting them together. All pieces must fit perfectly in order for the chassis to work. The chassis must be very strong to protect the driver if there is a crash. Crash bars are placed on the front of the vehicle to prevent damage to the inside parts such as the engine and transmission.

The body of the vehicle is the sheets or panels of metal that are attached to the chassis. In most classes of off-road racing, the chassis and body are not built by the team. The chassis and body of the off-road vehicle are made by manufacturers such as Jeep or Range Rover. The only exception is the Prototype Class in

expedition racing. In this class, the teams are allowed to create their own chassis and body.

The engines in an off-road race vehicle must be powerful. Off-road racers have large engines—a 500 horsepower V-8 engine. This gives the off-road vehicle enough power to go 134 miles per hour on rugged terrain. A larger engine lasts longer and is usually more reliable than a small-block engine. The fuel used in an off-road race vehicle is either gasoline or diesel fuel. If the driver is in an expedition race, diesel fuel is most often used since it works better in dusty or wet conditions.

*Most off-road vehicles look normal from the outside.*

# –Gigantic Tires

*Off-road* racing tires and wheels are larger than those on a regular car. This helps to keep the vehicle steady when going over rugged terrain. Four-wheel drive vehicles must have the same size tire on the front and rear wheels. They should also have the same brand and style of tire on the front and rear wheels. This helps the vehicle remain balanced and perform better.

A couple of important considerations with off-road tires is the tread and width of the tire. Aggressive treads, those with many grooves, are best for gripping the land. These are the type of tires most off-road racers use. However, aggressive tread tires wear out fast and they are noisy. Yet they are the best for mud and snow.

The width of the off-road tire is also important. Wider tires provide better flotation. This means they spread the vehicle's weight over a wider area. Wide tires are good for sand and light mud, but they are not so good for slippery snow.

Tire pressure, or how much air you put in the tire, can make a big difference in the performance of the car. The more pressure in the tire, the stiffer the tire becomes. If the off-road vehicle has a full load of supplies, the tire pressure should be at the maximum amount recommended, fully inflated to help support the heavy load.

Off-road tires wear out very quickly during a race. During a long expedition race, such as the Baja 1000 or Paris-Dakar Rally, tires are replaced several times with new tires that are kept in the supply vehicle. Teams also have supplies on hand to repair rips or holes in tires that still have plenty of tread left on them.

*Aggressively treaded tires are the best for mud or snow.*

# –What's a Winch

**When** competing in off-road racing, the terrain or land is often times muddy and slippery. Other than knowing how to drive well, the driver must be skilled with using a winch. The winch is a machine for hoisting a vehicle up in the air. It has a drum around which a rope or wire cable winds as the load is lifted.

There are two main types of winches. The electrically-operated are the most popular for off-road racers. The wire cable is operated from the vehicle's battery using a hand-held remote control.

The other type of winch is the mechanical winch. This winch has the same wire cable on a drum like the electrical winch, but it is driven by the engine and controlled using the accelerator (gas) pedal of the vehicle. Winching can be fun for the driver, but it is also very dangerous.

The wire cable is supporting the entire weight of the car. If the winch cable is not carefully positioned it can be destroyed by rocks or other sharp pieces, thus dropping the vehicle. For a standard off-road vehicle, an 8,000 pound winch is plenty. This means that the winch can hold a load of up to 8,000 pounds.

*Most races require that the vehicle be equipped with a winch for situations just like this.*

# —*Avoiding Trouble*

*There* are several items racers should carry in an off-road vehicle to help out if they get stuck in the mud or in another difficult situation. A sturdy off-road jack is important to carry. Most vehicles have jacks, but only a hydraulic jack or a heavy-duty mechanical jack are suited for off-road racing. A strong piece of wood should be carried in case the jack needs a level, flat surface.

A shovel is another important piece of equipment. Every off-road racer has gotten stuck at one time. A tow rope should be carried. This rope should be a long length since it may have to be attached to another vehicle in order to pull your vehicle out of a tough spot. Off-road racers should carry a lamp with a spare set of batteries.

A lamp will help light up an area so an off-road racer can work on a vehicle that has been damaged. A first-aid kit is also a very important item to carry. Add a pen, paper, adhesive tape, a mirror, and soap to the kit.

All off-road racers will be working on their vehicles during the race. A tool kit is a must for off-road racing. Some of the tools carried should include wrenches, pliers, a mole wrench,

screwdrivers, a hack-saw, and a hammer. Finally, a can of WD-40 is recommended to loosen rusted nuts, bolts, and fasteners.

One of the most important skills in off-road racing is knowing how to read a map. Maps are particularly important during long races where drivers will be driving over mountain passes, through jungles, across deserts, and other difficult, unmarked terrain. Since many races take place both during the day and at night, drivers need to keep track of where they are in case they are the only ones on the trail at the time.

Experienced racers and teams do what is called "pre-running." This means they drive the course ahead of time to find out where the obstacles are. They mark the dangerous areas on the map so they know what to watch for during the race.

Ahead of the race, teams decide how far to go on each day. They try to anticipate difficulties on the route and plan for enough time to cross a river or a mountain. If you want to become an off-road racer, one of the most important skills you can work on now is learning to read and understand maps.

*Anything can go wrong during a race.*

# —*Joining the Club*

**One** of the best ways to begin off-road racing is joining a club. There are many good reasons to join a club. Clubs schedule the races and set the rules for racing, including what type of equipment is allowed on the vehicles.

Clubs also monitor the point scoring system and provide trophies and prize money for the winners. At the end of the racing season, the club announces the champion.

Besides running the races, clubs help members find parts they need to repair their vehicle and help give new members tips on off-road racing. Some clubs run driving schools that new members can attend, to learn how to off-road race.

Joining an off-road racing club is a good way to meet people who like to do the same thing you do—off-road race!

*Opposite page: Joining an off-road racing club is a good step for someone who wants to start racing.*

# –*Glossary*

**Accelerator Pedal** - The accelerator pedal is the gas pedal in a vehicle.

**Aggressive Treads** - Tires with many grooves and are best for gripping the land. These are the type of tires most off-road racers use.

**Body** - Sheet metal panels of the car which fit over the chassis. The body is hand-crafted most of the time.

**Boojum** - desert plants that are only found in Baja Mexico. These plants are the oldest living organisms in the Baja desert. Some are 600 years old.

**Cable** - A strong, large-diameter heavy steel or fiber rope.

**Chassis** - The frame of the car. The chassis is like a skeleton of the car.

**Expedition** - An expedition is a journey taken by an organized group of people.

**Expedition Racing** - This kind of off-road racing is believed to be the toughest. Drivers are pushed to the limit in a test of endurance over several days and thousands of miles.

**Four-Wheel Drive** - The power from the engine is sent to all four wheels of the vehicle. In regular cars, the engine power is just sent to two of the four wheels, either front-wheel drive or rear-wheel drive.

**Inspection** - All cars must pass requirements for the height, weight, and equipment used in and on the vehicle. Vehicles are sometimes inspected before and after the race.

**Jack** - a device for raising heavy objects, such as cars and trucks.

**Jeep** - A vehicle which the Army called "G.P.," meaning "general purpose." A soldier started calling the vehicle "jeep" and the name stuck.

**Pre-Running** - Experienced racers and teams do what is called "pre-running." This means they drive the course ahead of time to find out where the obstacles are. They mark the dangerous areas on the map so they know what to watch for during the race.

**Production Vehicles** - These are vehicles that are driven on the streets everyday. Examples are Jeeps, Landcruisers and Land Rovers.

**Roll Bar** - An upside down wide "U" shaped bar that is very strong and is padded with foam to protect the driver's head. The roll bar is fitted to the chassis. It is required to be several inches above the driver's helmet. If a car crashes and flips over during a race, the weight of the car will be on the roll bar, not the driver.

**Team Spirit** - A team that works well together, and keeps the best attitude and spirit throughout the race. Many times an award is given to a team who has the best team spirit.

**Tire Pressure** - The amount of air that is put in the tire.

**Winch** - A winch is a machine for hoisting a vehicle up in the air. It has a drum around which a rope or wire cable winds as the load is lifted.

# —*Internet Sites*

### Formula 1 Links Heaven
http://ireland.iol.ie/~roym/
This site includes official sites, latest news, drivers, teams, computer games, circuits, mailing lists. This site has sound and video, very colorful and interactive.

### Drag Racing on the net
http://www.lm.com/~hemi/
This is a cool and interactive sight with sound and fun photos.

### Indyphoto.com
http://www.indyphoto.com/index.htm
This award winning site has excellent photographs of Indy Cars and it is updated on a regular basis.

### MotorSports Image Online
http://www.msimage.com/index2.htm
This site gives you standings, results, schedules, teams, news, and a photo gallery.

### Extreme Off-Road Racing
http://www.calpoly.edu/~jcallan/
This site has pre-runners, chat rooms, videos, racing pictures, wrecks, links, and much more extreme off-road racing stuff.

These sites are subject to change. Go to your favorite search engine and type in car racing for more sites.

---

# *Pass It On*

Racing Enthusiasts: educate readers around the country by passing on information you've learned about car racing. Share your little-known facts and interesting stories. Tell others what your favorite kind of car is or who your favorite racer is. We want to hear from you!

To get posted on the ABDO & Daughters website, e-mail us at "sports@abdopub.com"

**Visit the ABDO & Daughter website at www.abdopub.com**

# –Index